Problem Solving

Grade 5

Written by **Christine Hood**

Illustrations by **Sheila Bailey**

An imprint of Sterling Children's Books

D1232252

This book belongs to

_____

FLASH KIDS, STERLING, and the distinctive Sterling logo are registered trademarks of
Sterling Publishing Co., Inc.

Published by Sterling Publishing Co., Inc.
387 Park Avenue South, New York, NY 10016
Text and illustrations © 2007 by Flash Kids
Distributed in Canada by Sterling Publishing
c/o Canadian Manda Group, 165 Dufferin Street
Toronto, Ontario, Canada M6K 3H6
Distributed in the United Kingdom by GMC Distribution Services
Castle Place, 166 High Street, Lewes, East Sussex, England BN7 1XU
Distributed in Australia by Capricorn Link (Australia) Pty. Ltd.
P.O. Box 704, Windsor, NSW 2756, Australia

All rights reserved. No part of this publication may be reproduced,
stored in a retrieval system, or transmitted, in any form or by any means,
electronic, mechanical, photocopying, recording, or otherwise,
without prior written permission from the publisher.

Sterling ISBN 978-1-4114-3474-5

Manufactured in Canada

Lot #:
8 10 9 7
07/16

For information about custom editions, special sales, premium and
corporate purchases, please contact Sterling Special Sales
Department at 800-805-5489 or specialsales@sterlingpublishing.com.

Cover design and production by Mada Design, Inc.

Dear Parent,

Learning to solve problems is one of the most important skills in math. *Problem Solving* will help your child to look at problems with a critical eye. This book includes fun activities that help your child use logic, estimate, and choose a method to solve a problem. To get the most from *Problem Solving*, follow these simple steps:

- Provide a comfortable and quiet place for your child to work.
- Encourage your child to work at his or her own pace.
- Help your child with the problems if he or she needs it.
- Offer lots of praise and support.
- Encourage your child to work independently to gain confidence in his or her problem solving skills.
- Allow your child to enjoy the fun actvities in this book.
- Most of all, remember that learning should be fun!

Visit us at *www.flashkidsbooks.com* for free downloads, informative articles, and valuable parent resources!

Polly's Pets

Read each problem carefully, then solve it. Show your work.

1. Polly's Pets has dogs, cats, snakes, birds, and mice for sale. Over the weekend, the following animals were sold: 12 cats, 9 dogs, 17 birds, 5 mice, and 10 snakes. What was the total number of legs of the animals sold?
   Name the two operations you will use to solve the problem:

   _____

   _____

   Answer: _____

2. There are 6 tomcats that weigh 12.5 pounds each. There are 10 dogs that weigh 16 pounds each and 8 snakes that weigh 5.7 pounds each. How many pounds do all the animals weigh together?
   Name the two operations you will use to solve the problem:

   _____

   _____

   Answer: _____

3. When Polly's Pets opened, there were 63 animals. In the morning 9 people bought animals. In the afternoon 3 people bought animals. Each person bought the same number of animals. There were 15 animals left. How many animals did each person buy?
   Name the two operations you will use to solve the problem:

   _____

   _____

   Answer: _____

To the Top

Read the clues. Then solve the problems.

Clues:
- Each problem has two steps.
- Use ( ) as your first step to close off two numbers.
- Use two operation signs (x, −, +, ÷).
- Use one equals sign (=).

Example:

2 _____ 5 _____ 13 _____ 36

Answer:

2 x (5 + 13) = 36

1. 5 _____ 5 _____ 5 _____ 2

2. 90 _____ 6 _____ 3 _____ 12

3. 120 _____ 20 _____ 3 _____ 60

4. 66 _____ 7 _____ 8 _____ 10

5. 100 _____ 35 _____ 10 _____ 75

6. 10 _____ 2 _____ 10 _____ 50

On the Road

Solve the problems.

1. When the Jones family left on vacation, their odometer read 17,409.
    At the end of the first day it read 18,233. At the end of the week it read 20,396.
    How many miles did they travel the first day? _____
    How many miles did they travel the first week? _____

2. Manny drove three times farther than Sean. Sean drove five times farther than
    Bianca. Bianca drove 120 miles.
    How many miles did Sean drive? _____
    How many miles did Manny drive? _____

3. Camp Reynolds is at 5,305 feet. Camp Condor is at 9,550 feet, close to the
    mountaintop. The mountaintop peaks at 11,225 feet.
    How many feet will campers have to hike to reach the mountaintop from Camp
    Reynolds? _____
    How many feet higher is Camp Condor than Camp Reynolds? _____

4. Lisa drove for 6 hours on Thursday
    and $5\frac{1}{2}$ hours on Friday. She drove
    at 65 miles per hour on Thursday
    and 70 miles per hour on Friday.
    How many miles did Lisa drive on
    Thursday? _____
    How many miles did Lisa drive
    altogether? _____

Beach Party

Some problems have more than one step. Carefully read each problem.
Then decide which steps you should take to solve it. Write the steps in order.

> Example: Each hot dog costs 75¢. Cherie has one $5 bill, three $1 bills,
> and four quarters. How many hot dogs can she buy?
> Step 1: Find out how much money Cherie has: $5.00 + $3.00 + $1.00 = $9.00
> Step 2: Divide $9.00 by the cost of one hot dog (75¢): $.75\overline{)9.00} = 12$
> Answer: Cherie can buy 12 hot dogs.

1. Jenna bought ice cream for 7 of her friends.
   Each cup of ice cream has 3 scoops.
   If each scoop cost 15¢, how much money did she spend?
   Step 1: _____
   Step 2: _____
   Answer: _____

2. Tessa used $\frac{5}{10}$ of her bucket of sand for the sandcastle.
   Josh used $\frac{12}{20}$ of his bucket of sand. Who used more sand?
   Step 1: _____
   Step 2: _____
   Answer: _____

3. Biff spent three times more minutes surfing than Lan.
   Lan spent half as many minutes as Corey. Corey spent 120
   minutes surfing. Who surfed the longest?
   Step 1: _____
   Step 2: _____
   Step 3: _____
   Answer: _____

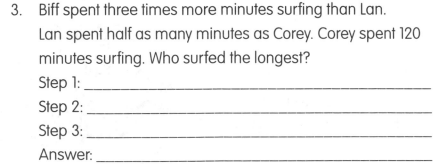

Fun with Fractions

Solve each fraction problem. Write the sum in its simplest form.

1. Luke ate $\frac{3}{4}$ of his steak. Jared ate $\frac{1}{3}$ of his steak. How much steak did they eat altogether?

_____

2. Nina baked 1 dozen cupcakes. She brought $\frac{2}{6}$ of them to school. What fraction of the cupcakes was left at home?

_____

3. Maria's team scored 24 points in the first half. She scored $\frac{3}{8}$ of those points. How many points did Maria score?

_____

4. $\frac{1}{4}$ of the puppies were black. $\frac{3}{6}$ of the puppies were brown. The rest were spotted. What fraction of the puppies were spotted?

_____

Ice Cream Combos

You can pick any two toppings you want at Ally's Ice Cream Shop. The topping choices are: gummy bears, chocolate chips, banana chips, candy sprinkles, hot caramel, peanuts, and whipped cream. List the possible topping combinations.

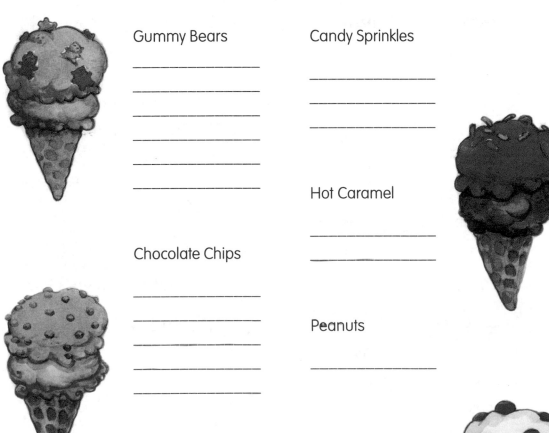

Gummy Bears

_____
_____
_____
_____
_____
_____

Chocolate Chips

_____
_____
_____
_____

Banana Chips

_____
_____
_____
_____

Candy Sprinkles

_____
_____
_____

Hot Caramel

_____
_____

Peanuts

_____

Measuring Up

Fill in each recipe card to show how much
of each ingredient is needed.

Chocolate Cupcakes

Ingredients	1 dozen	5 dozen	12 dozen	15 dozen
shortening	1 cup			
sugar	$1\frac{1}{3}$ cups			
eggs	2			
flour	$3\frac{1}{2}$ cups			
vanilla	2 tsp.			
baking soda	$1\frac{1}{4}$ tsp.			
chocolate chips	$1\frac{3}{4}$ cups			

Pink Lemonade

Ingredients	1 gallon	3 gallons	6 gallons	9 gallons
water	$5\frac{1}{2}$ cups			
sugar	$1\frac{2}{3}$ cups			
lemons	6			
food coloring	$\frac{1}{4}$ tsp.			

Climber's Challenge

Read the clues. Then solve the problems.

Clues:

- Each problem has two steps.

- Use ( ) as your first step to close off two numbers.

- Use two operation signs (x, −, +, ÷).

- Use one equals sign (=).

1. 120 _____ 12 _____ 15 _____ 150

2. 65 _____ 16 _____ 3 _____ 17

3. 76 _____ 14 _____ 2 _____ 31

4. 72 _____ 12 _____ 3 _____ 18

5. 20 _____ 8 _____ 13 _____ 124

6. 53 _____ 28 _____ 100 _____ 4

What's Probable?

Probability tells how likely it is that something will happen.

It is usually shown as a fraction.

Probability (P) = $\dfrac{\textbf{number of favorable outcomes}}{\textbf{number of all possible outcomes}}$

Example:

Probability of hitting a B = P(B) = $\dfrac{2}{6}$ = $\dfrac{1}{3}$

What is the probability of each problem?
Write answers in their simplest forms.

1. P(4) = _____

2. P(odd number) = _____

3. P(G) = _____

4. P(A or E) = _____

5. P(heart or star) = _____

6. P(pentagon) = _____

7. P(striped) = _____

8. P(white or black) = _____

Climber's Challenge

Read the clues. Then solve the problems.

Clues:

• Each problem has two steps.

• Use ( ) as your first step to close off two numbers.

• Use two operation signs (x, −, +, ÷).

• Use one equals sign (=).

1. 120 _____ 12 _____ 15 _____ 150

    2. 65 _____ 16 _____ 3 _____ 17

        3. 76 _____ 14 _____ 2 _____ 31

            4. 72 _____ 12 _____ 3 _____ 18

                5. 20 _____ 8 _____ 13 _____ 124

                    6. 53 _____ 28 _____ 100 _____ 4

What's Probable?

Probability tells how likely it is that something will happen.

It is usually shown as a fraction.

Probability (P) = $\dfrac{\textbf{number of favorable outcomes}}{\textbf{number of all possible outcomes}}$

Example:

Probability of hitting a B = P(B) = $\dfrac{2}{6}$ = $\dfrac{1}{3}$

What is the probability of each problem?
Write answers in their simplest forms.

1. P(4) = _____

2. P(odd number) = _____

3. P(G) = _____

4. P(A or E) = _____

5. P(heart or star) = _____

6. P(pentagon) = _____

7. P(striped) = _____

8. P(white or black) = _____

School Survey

Kayla did a school survey to find out what kinds of pets students have.
She put her results in a circle graph. Read the circle graph

Number of Pets

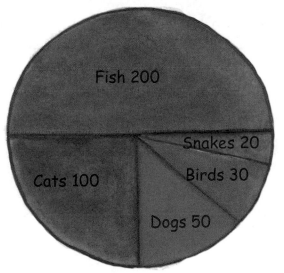

Fish 200

Snakes 20

Birds 30

Cats 100

Dogs 50

1. How many dogs do students have? _____

2. How many snakes or birds do students have? _____

3. What fraction of the pets are fish? _____

4. What fraction of the pets are fish or cats? _____

5. What percentage of the pets are dogs, snakes, or birds? _____

6. How many total pets do students have? _____

In the Band

Read each problem carefully. Then solve it.

Round up or down to the next whole number, if needed.

1. There are 130 students in the school band. Of these band members, 20% play brass instruments. How many students do not play brass instruments? _____

2. There are 28 students who play woodwind instruments. 35% of these students play the clarinet. How many students play the clarinet? _____

3. Each band member must put in $50.00 at the beginning of the year. Of this money, 65% goes toward cleaning the uniforms.
   How much money is spent on cleaning each student's uniform? _____
   How much money is spent on cleaning all students' uniforms? _____

4. The percussion section has snare drums, kettledrums, bass drums, and xylophones. Of the 40 students in the percussion section, 45% play snares, 12% play kettles, and 25% play bass.
   What percent of students in the percussion section play xylophone? _____
   How many students play each instrument?
   Snares: _____   Kettles: _____
   Bass: _____   Xylophone: _____

What Are My Chances?

Read each problem carefully. Then solve it.

1. Jessica has 10 marbles in her bag. 5 marbles are red, 2 are green, 2 are purple, and 1 is yellow. She is reaching into the bag to choose a marble.

   What is the probability of choosing a green or purple marble? _____

   What is the probability of choosing a red marble? _____

2. Eight students are in the study group: Emma, Erik, Connor, Shelby, Huma, Emily, Cris, and Heather. They are drawing their names from a hat.

   P(names that begin with E) = _____

   P(names that begin with C or H) = _____

   P(names that begin with S) = _____

3. The spinner tells which color shirts students will wear for the school fair.

   P(green) = _____

   P(blue or pink) = _____

   P(white) = _____

Shifty Shapes

Congruent figures have the same shape and size.

2"
2"

1. Are these shapes congruent?   YES   NO

Explain your answer:

_____

_____

2. Are these shapes congruent?   YES   NO

Explain your answer:

_____

_____

6 m
6 cm

3. Are these shapes congruent?   YES   NO

Explain your answer:

_____

_____

4. Are these shapes congruent?   YES   NO

Explain your answer:

_____

_____

Draw a congruent shape next to each shape below.

5.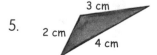
3 cm
2 cm
4 cm

6.

Money Matters

Read each problem carefully. Then solve it.
Round up or down if needed.

1. Coach Drew collected $16.50 from the soccer players and $22.75 from the tennis players. There are 15 soccer players and 24 tennis players. How much money did he collect? _____

2. There were 1,484 students eating lunch in the cafeteria today. Of these students, 25% bought spaghetti for $2.35, 50% bought sandwiches for $1.75, and the rest bought meatloaf for $1.99. How much money did the cafeteria collect? _____

3. Jason mows 6 lawns each weekend to make extra money. He makes $2.25 per lawn. He is saving to buy a new bike, which costs $165.99. If Jason has worked 3 weekends, how many more does he need to work to buy the bike? _____

4. The charity event raised $9,753. The money must be equally divided between a homeless shelter, a library, and an animal shelter. How much money will each organization get? _____

Weathering the Averages

Read each problem carefully. Then solve it. Round up or down as needed.

1. A huge snowstorm hit the city last week. On Monday, 18 inches fell. On Tuesday, 12 inches fell. On both Wednesday and Thursday, 16 inches fell. Finally, on Friday, 26 inches fell.

    What was the average snowfall for the first three days? _____

    What was the average snowfall for the week? _____

2. This summer is incredibly hot! On one day the temperature went from 70° to 108° Fahrenheit! At 8:00 AM, the temperature was 70°. Over the next 6 hours, the temperature rose to 75°, 83°, 92°, 99°, 103°, and finally, 108°.

    What was the average temperature between 8:00 AM and 11:00 AM? _____

    What was the average temperature between the lowest and highest temperature that day? _____

3. Rainfall averages change every year. Over the years 2000 to 2004, Middleton experienced the following rainfall measurements, in order: 16.2, 9.3, 10.5, 18.9, and 13.1.

    What was the rainfall in 2001? _____

    What was the average rainfall of 2000, 2002, and 2004? _____

    What was the average rainfall for these five years? _____

Averages for Kids

Read each problem carefully. Then solve it. Round up or down as needed.

1. Carla ran the sprint in 10.4 seconds. Tanya ran the sprint in 11.3 seconds. Jake and Sara tied at 9.7 seconds. Kim came in at 10.8 seconds. Mason beat everyone with a time of 9.2 seconds.

    Who took the longest to run the sprint? _____

    What is the difference between the fastest and slowest times? _____

    What is the average time run by all sprinters? _____

2. Brandon is 1.78 meters tall. His brother Jamie is 1.83 meters tall. The twins Brad and Jennifer are both 1.14 meters tall. Their sister Selena is 1.91 meters tall!

    What is the average height of all the boys? _____

    What is the average height of all the brothers and sisters? _____

3. In his last six basketball games, Sam made 30% of all points scored by his team. The total points scored were: 112, 89, 95, 77, 103, and 92.

    What was the average total score of all six games? _____

    On average, how many points did Sam score in each of the last six games?

    _____

Dessert Table

The Keller sisters each ordered dessert after dinner. They ordered a sundae, cheesecake, peach cobbler, and chocolate cake.

Use the clues to match Ariel, Anna, Ashlee, and Alicia with their desserts.

Ashlee's dessert is very cold.

The name of Ariel's dessert begins with a "C."

Alicia's dessert has lots of icing.

	cheesecake	chocolate cake	peach cobbler	sundae
Ariel				
Anna				
Ashlee				
Alicia				

Favorite Sports

Karina did a survey of the 40 students in her class to find out their favorite sports.
She recorded her results in a pie chart.

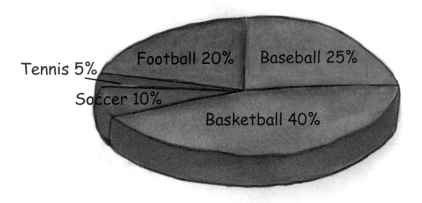

How many students like each sport the best?

Baseball _____

Football _____

Tennis _____

Soccer _____

Basketball _____

Super Chefs!

Tana and her friends are having a cooking party. To help everyone with measurements, Tana posted this chart.

8 ounces (oz.) = 1 cup

16 ounces (oz.) = 1 pound

2 cups = 1 pint (pt.)

2 pints = 1 quart (qt.)

4 quarts = 1 gallon

3 teaspoons (tsp.) = 1 tablespoon (Tbs.)

8 oz — 1 cup
4 oz — ½ cup
2 oz — ¼ cup

SUGAR
16 oz = 1 lb

1. Ben is making 3 gallons of lemonade. He needs $2\frac{1}{2}$ cups of sugar for each gallon.

   How many ounces of sugar does Ben need?_____

   How many total cups of lemonade is he making?_____

2. Ella added 9 Tbs. of vanilla to her triple batch of chocolate chip cookies. Then she tripled the batch again.

   How many teaspoons of vanilla does she need for all six batches? _____

   How many teaspoons of vanilla would she need for only two batches? _____

3. Manuel is making a $\frac{1}{4}$-pound burger for each friend in the group. There are 12 friends.

   How many ounces of ground beef are in each burger? _____

   How many pounds of ground beef does he need? _____

4. Zoe is adding 2 pints more tomato sauce to her soup than Marco. Marco is adding 3 cups less to his soup than Olivia. Olivia is adding 5 cups to her soup.

   How many cups of tomato sauce is Zoe adding to her soup? _____

   How many ounces is Marco adding to his soup? _____

5. Devon needs $8\frac{1}{2}$ pounds of cheese for all 16 pizzas.

   How many ounces of cheese does he need? _____

   If he makes $\frac{1}{4}$ as many pizzas, how many ounces will he need? _____

6. The recipe for one apple pie calls for $\frac{3}{4}$ tsp. cinnamon. Patti is making 6 apple pies.

   How many tsp. of cinnamon does she need? _____

   Patti is using $7\frac{1}{2}$ tsp. cinnamon. How many pies is she making? _____

Shapes and Numbers

Read the clues to find the correct number.

1. It is not an even number.
    It is in the square and the triangle.
    It is more than 12.
    What is the number? _____

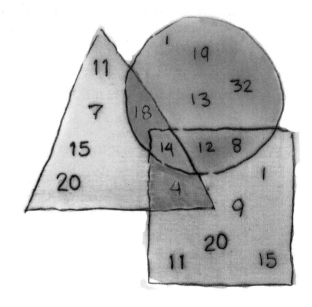

2. It is an even number.
    It is not in the rectangle.
    It is divisible by 6.
    What is the number? _____

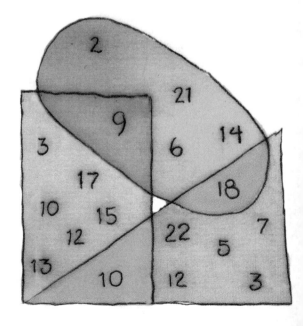

Batting Order

Carrie, Jess, Aimee, Tye, Tammy, and Derek are waiting in line to bat.

- Jess is right in front of Aimee.

- Derek is between Tammy and Aimee.

- Jess is looking ahead at Tye, who is next up to bat.

- Three people are standing between Jess and Carrie.

Write the order the batters are standing in line.

_____

_____

_____

_____

_____

_____

Watch the Clock

Read each problem carefully. Then solve it.

1. Nola's train left the station at 10:45 AM. She arrived at Silver Station at 2:35 PM and switched trains. The second train left Silver Station at 2:50 PM and arrived at Red Rock Station at 6:35 PM. How long was Nola on the train?

    _____ hours   _____ minutes

2. The cruise ship left port at 2:15 PM. It arrived in Ensenada, Mexico, at 7:40 AM the next morning. How long did the ship sail?

    _____ hours   _____ minutes

3. Teddie started skiing at 8:25 in the morning. He took a break for lunch from noon to 1:10 PM. Then he skied the rest of the day until the lifts closed at 6:00 PM. How long did Teddie ski?

    _____ hours   _____ minutes

4. Michele works at the market from 9:30 AM to 12:00 PM each weekday. She makes $2.85 per hour. She is saving every penny! When she checked her bank to see how much she had saved, she counted $176.70. How many hours and minutes has she worked to save this amount?

    _____ hours   _____ minutes

Math Magic

Read the rules, then fill in the missing numbers in the magic squares.

Here are the rules:

• You can't use a number more than once.

• All columns and rows must add up to the same number.

1. All columns and rows add up to 15.

10		2
0		
5	4	

2. All columns and rows add up to 18.

	6	9
10		
5		1

3. All columns and rows add up to 20.

4		3
	7	
		9

4. All columns and rows add up to 21.

	5	
11		3
		8

Right on Schedule

Read the bus schedule below. Then answer the questions.

Buses	A	B	C	D	E
Delaware	8:05	8:40	9:15	10:10	11:30
Chatham	8:15	8:50	9:25	10:20	11:40
Willam	8:55	9:30	10:05	11:00	12:20
Rainfall	9:30	10:05	10:40	11:35	12:55
Tyler	11:48	12:33	1:08	2:03	3:23
Shasta	12:02	12:47	1:22	2:17	3:37
Fairmont	1:25	2:00	2:35	3:30	4:50

1. How long does it take to get from Chatham to Tyler? _____

2. If you miss Bus A from Shasta, how long do you have to wait for the next bus? _____

3. How long does it take to get from Willam to Fairmont? _____

4. You took Bus C from Delaware to Rainfall. Then you picked up Bus E to Shasta. How long did you spend on the bus? _____

5. You took Bus A from Chatham to Shasta. Then you picked up Bus D to Fairmont. How long did you have to wait for Bus D? _____

6. Bus B picked you up in Willam and dropped you off in Tyler. You picked up Bus E to get home to Shasta. How long did you wait for Bus E? _____

7. How much time is there in Rainfall between Bus A and Bus E? _____

8. How much time is there in Fairmont between Bus B and Bus D?_____

Bank Account

Cameron just opened a bank account. Read all the deposits and debits listed below. Then fill out the bankbook on the next page. The first entry has been done for you.

- On August 12, Cameron opened his bank account with $85.50.

- On August 16, he deposited allowance money for $13.75.

- On August 28, he bought a new skateboard for $35.99.

- On September 12, he bought school supplies for $12.00.

- On September 15, he bought two new shirts and a pair of jeans for $24.55.

- On September 19, he deposited his birthday check for $20.00.

- On October 5, he bought his mom a new watch for $15.75.

- On October 18, he bought new skateboarding helmet for $14.50.

Fill in the bankbook below.

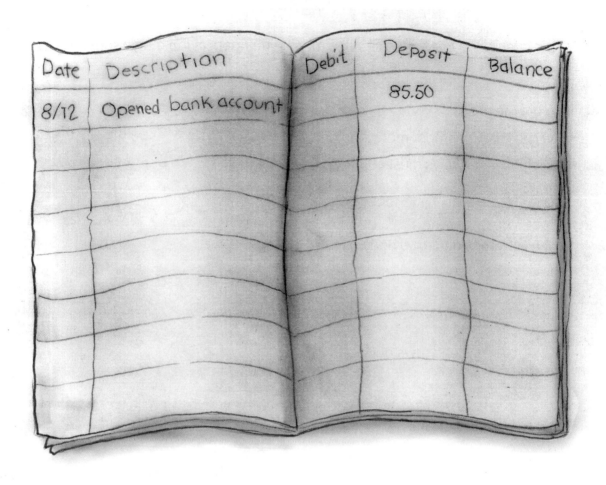

Date	Description	Debit	Deposit	Balance
8/12	Opened bank account		85.50	

1. What were Cameron's total debits? _____

2. What were Cameron's total deposits? _____

3. What is Cameron's ending balance as of October 18? _____

More Math Magic

Read the rules, then fill in the missing numbers in the magic squares.

Here are the rules:

• You can't use a number more than once.

• All columns and rows must add up to the same number.

1. All columns and rows add up to 18.

3	7	
	5	9

2. All columns and rows add up to 24.

	11	
9		3
10	1	

3. All columns and rows add up to 26.

12		4
		17
14		

4. All columns and rows add up to 34.

14	11		
	16		3
7		12	
4		15	10

Fraction Follies

Problems need to include enough information for you to solve them. Read each problem carefully. If there is enough information, solve the problem. If there isn't, put an X on the line. Then tell what is missing.

1. Jasmine made 2 dozen brownies for her dad's birthday. Her dad ate $\frac{1}{4}$ dozen on Tuesday, $\frac{3}{4}$ dozen on Thursday, and $\frac{5}{8}$ dozen on Friday. How many brownies were leftover? _____

   What's missing? _____

   _____

2. Wyatt ate $\frac{6}{10}$ of his bag of popcorn, Brianna ate $\frac{4}{5}$ of her bag, Tana ate $\frac{2}{3}$ of her bag, and Jeremy ate $\frac{2}{6}$ of his bag. How many bags of popcorn did they eat altogether? _____

   What's missing? _____

   _____

3. Each baseball team has 9 players. On game day, $\frac{1}{3}$ of the players on all the teams don't show up. How many teams can be formed from the leftover players?

   _____

   What's missing? _____

   _____

4. Troy kicked $\frac{1}{3}$ of all the soccer goals scored in the last eight games. His team's scores were as follows: 5, 8, 2, 6, 4, 5, 9. How many total points did Troy score? (Round up or down as needed.) _____

   What's missing? _____

Mall Mania

What did these children buy at the mall? Read the clues to find out.
Then fill in the chart.

- Hanna ate what she bought for dessert.

- What Aaron bought begins with a "T."

- Staci bought something she will wear every day.

- None of the kids bought anything that starts with the first letter in their names.

	tennis shoes	skateboard	ice cream	watch	bike
Brett					
Hanna					
Scott					
Aaron					
Staci					

Basketball Tournament

Read the problem carefully. Then answer the question.
It may help you to draw a chart or make a list.

Danny's team, the Spartans, entered the all-district basketball tournament.

- In the first round, all 16 teams played each of the other teams. The 8 teams who won the most games played in the second round.

- In the second round, all 8 teams played each of the other teams. The 4 teams who won the most games played in the semifinals.

- In the semifinals, each of the 4 teams played one game. The winner of these two games played in the finals.

- The Spartans played in the finals and won the game and the tournament.

How many total games of basketball did the Spartans play? _____

At the Aquarium

Several fifth-grade classes went on a trip to the new city aquarium. They saw 200 different fish and mammals. Back in class, Mr. Cline classified the animals by group in a pie chart.

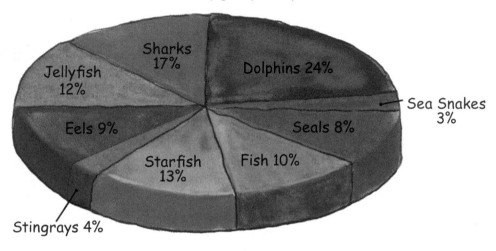

Sharks 17%

Dolphins 24%

Jellyfish 12%

Sea Snakes 3%

Eels 9%

Seals 8%

Starfish 13%

Fish 10%

Stingrays 4%

How many of each animal or fish were in the aquarium? (Hint: Round up or down as needed.)

Dolphins _____

Sea Snakes _____

Fish _____

Sharks _____

Jellyfish _____

Seals _____

Stingrays _____

Starfish _____

Eels _____

Guess the Shape

Read the clues and guess the shape.

1. I have no corners.
    I have round ends.
    I have two long sides.
    What shape am I? _____

2. I am a polygon.
    I have straight sides.
    I have eight sides.
    What shape am I? _____

3. I have three sides.
    All my angles are the same.
    I am a triangle.
    What kind of triangle am I? _____

4. I have four sides.
    All my angles are 90°.
    I am not three-dimensional.
    What shape am I? _____

Road Rules

Read the problem and compare the distances.
Then answer the questions. Round up or down as needed.

Emmett lives in Appleton. He will be driving through all of these towns on the same road:

- Mountville is 230.7 miles further than Junction.

- Chaney is 75.5 miles further than Mountville.

- Sun City is 56.2 miles closer than Junction.

- Danville is 83.6 miles further than Sun City.

- Faith is 36.8 miles closer than Sun City.

- Junction is 102.3 miles away.

1. Write the city names in order, from closest to furthest from Appleton.
    Write the mileage next to each city.

    _____

    _____

    _____

    _____

    _____

    _____

2. How many miles is it from Junction to Chaney? _____

3. How many miles is it from Mountville to Faith? _____

4. How many miles is it from Sun City to Danville? _____

5. Emmett drove from Danville to Chaney. Then he drove back to Sun City. How many miles did he drive? _____

6. Emmett drove from Faith to Junction. In the morning, he left for Mountville, but only made it halfway there before running out of gas. How many miles did he drive? _____

7. After Emmett filled up his car with gas, he finished his drive to Mountville. From there, he went to Chaney, and then drove all the way back home to Appleton. How many miles did he drive? _____

Fraction Puzzles

Write a number sentence for each picture. Then solve the problem.
Change fractions to mixed numbers, if needed. Hint: Write fractions to represent the shaded part of each picture.

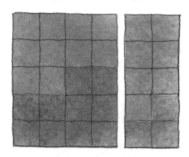

1.

_____ + _____ = _____

2.

_____ + _____ = _____

3.

_____ + _____ = _____

4.

_____ + _____ = _____

Favorite Hobbies

Hector and his friends all have different hobbies.
Read the clues to find out who has each hobby and where they are sitting.
Write the names and hobbies on the lines around the globe.

The children are:

Hector

Anh

Nicki

Hassan

The hobbies are:

cooking

singing

mountain climbing

biking

Clues:

1. A boy whose name begins with "H" loves nature. He is sitting to Nicki's left.

2. Nicki is not sitting next to the boy who likes to cook.

3. Anh does not like singing or cooking.

4. Hassan does not like mountain climbing.

_____

_____

_____   _____ Nicki

_____   _____

_____

_____

Perfect Patterns

Can you guess the patterns? Write the rule for each pattern.
Then fill in the missing numbers. (Hint: Read the patterns from left to right.)

1.

108	9
144	
36	3
	11

Rule: _____

2.

3	18
	60
37	52
15	

Rule: _____

3.

5	100
20	400
8	
	60

Rule: _____

4.

99	
	13
50	37
35	22

Rule: _____

Picking a Pool

Jessica's family is building a pool in the backyard. They can't decide which shape and size to build. Figure out the perimeter of each pool. Then answer the question.

Pool A

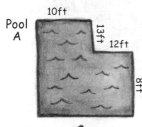

10ft
13ft
12ft
8ft

What is the perimeter of this pool? _____

Pool B

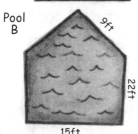

9ft
22ft
15ft

What is the perimeter of this pool? _____

Pool C

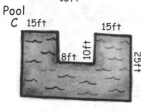

15ft   15ft
8ft 10ft   25ft

What is the perimeter of this pool? _____

Pool D

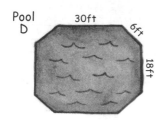

30ft   6ft
18ft

What is the perimeter of this pool? _____

Which pool would fit best in a backyard that is 20 feet at the top and bottom and 32 feet on both sides? _____

Why? _____

Football Fanatics

Here are some facts about football:

Touchdown = 6 points
Football field = 100 yards
Field goal = 3 points
Players on each team = 11
Safety = 2 points

First down = 10 yards
4 quarters in a game
Line of scrimmage = where a
play begins

Every time a team scores a touchdown, it gets a chance to kick one extra point.

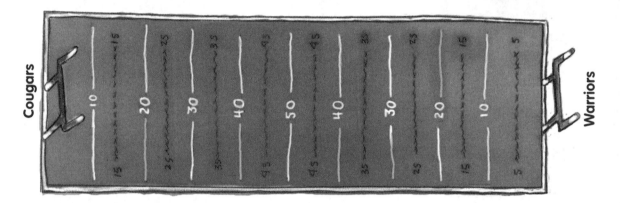

Solve these problems about the game of football.

1. The Cougars scored 5 touchdowns in the game. They missed 2 of their extra points. The Warriors scored 3 touchdowns and 3 field goals. They made all of their extra points.
   Who won the game? _____
   What was the final score? Cougars _____ Warriors _____

2. The Warriors are on their own 45 yard line. The running back carried the ball to the Cougar's 30 yard line.
   How many yards did the running back run? _____
   What percentage of the field did he cover? _____

3. The line of scrimmage was on the Cougar's own 32 yard line. The wide receiver caught the ball at the 50 yard line and ran 16 more yards.
How many yards did he gain? _____
On what yard line did the receiver end up?

_____

4. The game went as follows:

	1st quarter	2nd quarter	3rd quarter	4th quarter
Cougars	1 touchdown 1 extra point 2 field goals	3 field goals	1 safety	2 touchdowns 1 extra point
Warriors	2 touchdowns 2 extra points	2 field goals	2 touchdowns 1 extra point	1 field goal 1 safety

Who was ahead at halftime (after the second quarter)? _____

Who won the game? _____

What was the final score?

Cougars: _____

Warriors: _____

5. The Cougars' quarterback ran from his own 46 yard line to the Warriors' 45 yard line.
Did he make the first down? _____

How many yards did he run? _____

6. In three games, Cougar quarterback Justin Craig threw for 336 yards and 5 touchdowns, 217 yards and 2 touchdowns, and 295 yards and 4 touchdowns. Warrior quarterback Bill Dawson threw for 258 yards and 3 touchdowns, 312 yards and 2 touchdowns, and 322 yards and 4 touchdowns. (Remember, a touchdown is worth 6 points.)

What was the average yardage thrown by both quarterbacks? _____

What was the average score made by both quarterbacks? _____

Map It!

Study the map. Then answer the questions on the next page.

Round up or down as needed.

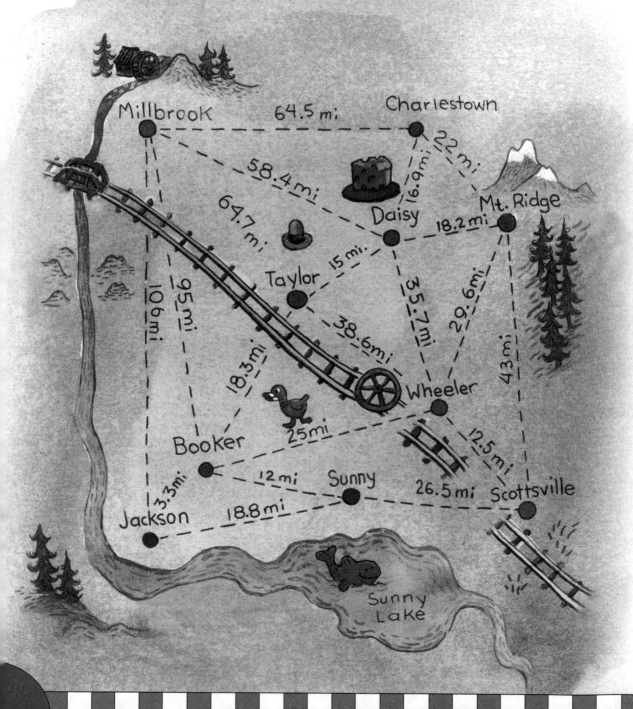

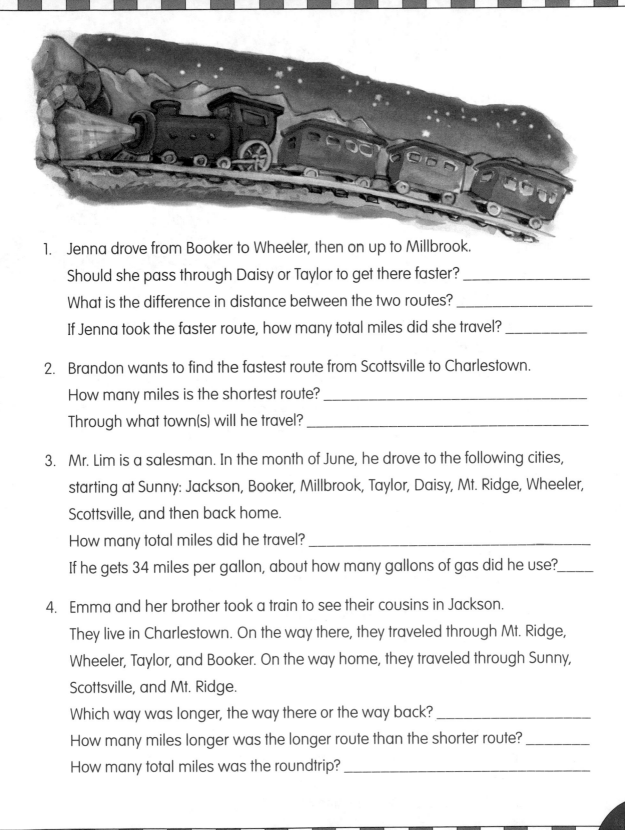

1. Jenna drove from Booker to Wheeler, then on up to Millbrook.
   Should she pass through Daisy or Taylor to get there faster? _____
   What is the difference in distance between the two routes? _____
   If Jenna took the faster route, how many total miles did she travel? _____

2. Brandon wants to find the fastest route from Scottsville to Charlestown.
   How many miles is the shortest route? _____
   Through what town(s) will he travel? _____

3. Mr. Lim is a salesman. In the month of June, he drove to the following cities,
   starting at Sunny: Jackson, Booker, Millbrook, Taylor, Daisy, Mt. Ridge, Wheeler,
   Scottsville, and then back home.
   How many total miles did he travel? _____
   If he gets 34 miles per gallon, about how many gallons of gas did he use?_____

4. Emma and her brother took a train to see their cousins in Jackson.
   They live in Charlestown. On the way there, they traveled through Mt. Ridge,
   Wheeler, Taylor, and Booker. On the way home, they traveled through Sunny,
   Scottsville, and Mt. Ridge.
   Which way was longer, the way there or the way back? _____
   How many miles longer was the longer route than the shorter route? _____
   How many total miles was the roundtrip? _____

All About Area

Use the formula to figure out the area for each problem:

Area = length x width.

1. Grandpa Joe planted three gardens in his backyard:
    The flower garden is 12 ft. x 8.2 ft.
    The vegetable garden is 17 ft. x 5.3 ft.
    The herb garden is 10.2 ft. x 9 ft.
    Which garden has the largest area?

    _____

    What is the area? _____ sq. ft.
    What is the difference in square feet between the largest garden
    and the smallest garden? _____ sq. ft.
    What is the total area of all three gardens? _____ sq. ft.

2. Fairmont Elementary is adding four new classrooms:
    Classroom A: 25 ft. x 35 ft.   Classroom B: 21 ft. x 40.5 ft.
    Classroom C: 32 ft. x 50 ft.   Classroom D: 40.5 ft. x 40 ft.
    Which classroom has the largest area? _____
    What is the area? _____sq. ft.
    Which classroom has the smallest area? _____
    What is the area? _____ sq. ft.
    What is the total area of all four classrooms? _____ sq. ft.

3. Keisha is knitting scarves for her friends:
    The blue scarf is 6.5 in. x 38 in.
    The purple scarf is 12 in. x 30 in.
    The red scarf is 8.5 in. x 36 in.
    The green scarf is 5 in. x 48.3 in.
    Which scarf has the largest area? _____ What is the area? _____ sq. in.
    What is the difference in square inches between the biggest scarf and the
    smallest scarf? _____ sq. in.
    What is the total area Keisha knitted? _____ sq. in.

Racquetball Championship

Zane and 23 other players entered the all-city racquetball championship.
This is what happened.

Round 1: Each player played all the other players.
The 12 players who won the most games moved on to the second round.

Round 2: Each player played all the other players.
The 4 players who won the most games moved on to the third round.

Round 3: Each player played only one game.
The winners of these two games played in the last game, the championship round.

Championship Round: Zane played Alyssa in the championship round.
Unfortunately, he lost by 2 points.

How many games did Zane play? _____

Raffle Graph

Mrs. Wu's fifth-grade class is selling raffle tickets to sponsor the Furry Friends Animal Shelter. She kept track of ticket sales on a line graph.

Read the information on the graph below.
Then answer the questions on the next page.

_____	Boys
- - - -	Girls

Raffle Ticket Sales

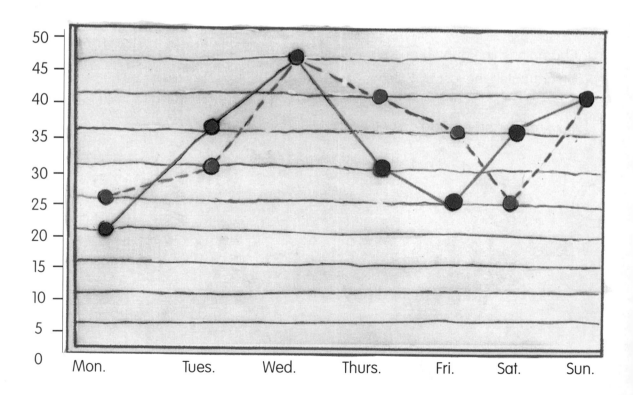

1. Who sold more tickets, boys or girls? _____

   How many more tickets did they sell?_____

2. How many more tickets were sold on Wednesday than Friday?_____

3. Which two days did boys and girls sell the same number of tickets?_____

   _____

4. Which day had the lowest number of sales? _____

   How many fewer tickets were sold on this day than the day with the highest

   number of sales? _____

5. Which two days had the same number of sales?_____

6. If each raffle ticket cost $2.50, how much money did the children raise for the

   animal shelter?_____

7. Of the money that was raised 45% went to dogs, 35% went to cats, and 20%

   went to rabbits. How much did each type of animal get?

   Dogs: _____

   Cats: _____

   Rabbits: _____

Tie-Dye T-Shirts

For the school fair, your booth is making tie-dye T-shirts. Students can choose two fun colors for each T-shirt. A variety of colors are available: ruby red, purple grape, ocean blue, leafy green, sunny yellow, cheeky pink, chocolate brown, burnt orange, and black cat.

Cassie is making a sign to show all the different color combinations.
Help her by filling in all the possible combinations.

Ruby Red

———————————
———————————
———————————
———————————
———————————
———————————
———————————
———————————

Purple Grape

———————————
———————————
———————————
———————————
———————————
———————————
———————————

Ocean Blue

———————————
———————————
———————————
———————————
———————————
———————————

Leafy Green

———————————
———————————
———————————
———————————
———————————

Sunny Yellow

———————————
———————————
———————————

Cheeky Pink

———————————
———————————

Chocolate Brown

———————————

Burnt Orange

———————————

How many fun color combinations are available?

———————————————————————————————————

Tall, Taller, Tallest

Compare the height of each boy. Then answer the questions.

Tanner is $5\frac{1}{2}$ inches taller than Randy. Randy is $16\frac{1}{2}$ inches taller than Dylan. Brian is 5 inches shorter than Dylan. Kevin is $8\frac{1}{2}$ inches shorter than Tanner. Dylan is 4 feet, 5 inches tall.

1. Write the boys' names in order, from tallest to shortest.

   _____ _____ _____ _____ _____

2. How tall is Brian? _____

3. How tall is Tanner? _____

4. How many inches taller is Randy than Kevin? _____

5. How much taller is the tallest boy than the shortest boy? _____

6. How many feet and inches tall are all the boys put together? _____

Pet Supplies

Read the paragraph and answer the questions.

Neena has 6 cats. She is making a trip to the pet store to buy them some treats and toys. She made a special list for each cat, but then mixed up the lists. Use the clues below to help Neena match the correct list with each cat. She used a $5 bill to pay for each cat's items.

Item	
brush	75¢
catnip mouse	75¢
tasty treats	50¢
sleeping mat	99¢
scratching post	86¢
jingle balls	35¢
toy feather	70¢
claw clipper	48¢
meow munchies	32¢

- Spike needs some things for his claws. Neena got $1.66 in change.

- Sheena got the same number of catnip mice as Rocky. Neena got $2.08 in change.

- Thor likes to snack all the time. Neena got 27¢ in change.

- Rocky loves toys more than any other cat. Neena got 52¢ in change.

- Prissy needs one of everything, except a sleeping mat. Neena got 89¢ in change.

- Mouse only needs five things, but three times as many tasty treats as Sheena. Neena got 1¢ in change.

List 1 _____
✓ scratching post
2 catnip mice
1 claw clipper
1 tasty treats

List 2 _____
1 brush
1 catnip mouse
1 tasty treats
1 scratching post
1 jingle balls
1 toy feather
1 claw clipper
1 meow munchies

List 3 _____
2 catnip mice
6 jingle balls
4 toy feathers
1 claw clipper

List 4 _____
1 meow munchies
1 sleeping mat
2 toy feathers
6 tasty treats
1 claw clipper

List 5 _____
2 tasty treats
2 catnip mice
1 meow munchies
1 toy feather

List 6 _____
4 tasty treats
1 brush
4 meow munchies
2 jingle balls

1. How much more did Thor's items cost than Sheena's? _____

2. How much did all the cats' items cost altogether? _____

3. After paying for all the items, how much money did Neena have leftover?

_____

Most and Least

Read each problem carefully. Then solve it. Use reduced fractions
or mixed numbers to show your answers, as needed.

1. Brent ate $\frac{5}{8}$ of his pizza. Tyler ate $\frac{3}{4}$ of her pizza.
   Grant ate $\frac{3}{10}$ of his pizza. Shane ate $\frac{4}{5}$ of his pizza.
   Who ate the most pizza? _____ Who ate the least pizza? _____
   How much more pizza did Tyler eat than Grant? _____
   How much pizza did the children eat altogether? _____
   Write who ate the most to the least pizza, in order:

   _____ _____ _____ _____

2. Shana scored 80% of 70 points. Justin scored 63% of 120 points.
   Erin scored 58% of 90 points. Myra scored 85% of 80 points.
   Who scored the most points? _____
   Who scored the least points? _____
   How many more points did Justin score
   than Shana? _____
   How many points did the children score
   altogether? _____
   Write who scored the least to the most points,
   in order:

   _____ _____ _____ _____

Find the Pattern

Can you guess the patterns? Write the rule for each pattern.

Then fill in the missing numbers. (Hint: Read the patterns from left to right.)

1.

13	25
	34
3	15
30	42
	77

Rule: _____

2.

15	
9	36
	48
20	80
11	44

Rule: _____

3.

10	12
	15
12	18
13	
14	24

Rule: _____

4.

6	18
	40
9	63
11	99
	143

Rule: _____

Using Variables

Variables can help you solve problems. Use variables to make equations and find the mystery numbers.

Example: Britney earned $12 per week at the bakery for an unknown number of weeks. She earned $84. How many weeks has she worked?

Equation: $12n = 84$ Answer: Britney has worked 7 weeks.

$84 \div 12 = 7$

Make an equation for each problem. Use a variable to represent the unknown number. Then solve the problem.

1. Theo drove 486 miles on 18 gallons of gas. How many miles per gallon did his car get?
    Equation: _____
    Answer: _____

2. Melissa scored 1,595 points on her tests for the year. Sam scored 1,408 points on his tests for the year. How many more points did Melissa score?
    Equation: _____
    Answer: _____

3. Mia took the train 15 miles both to and from work each day for an unknown number of days. At the end of this time, she had traveled 360 miles. How many days did she travel to and from work?
    Equation: _____   Answer: _____

4. Matt took 504 pictures with his new camera. He snapped a roll of pictures each day. He took pictures for 3 weeks. How many pictures were on each roll of film?
    Equation: _____   Answer: _____

Soccer Fans

Read about the soccer stadium. Then solve the problems.

The soccer stadium has 89,545 seats.
There are 530 more seats in special reserved boxes.

1. 75,844 regular tickets were sold for this weekend's game. In addition, 275 reserved box seats were sold.
   How many tickets are left?_____

2. In the regular sections, Section A holds 20,560 people. Section B holds exactly twice as many people as Section C. Section C holds 18,204 people. There are four sections.
   How many people does Section D hold?_____

3. 15,852 tickets were sold on Thursday for Sunday's game. Three times as many tickets were sold on Friday. But only half as many tickets were sold on Saturday as were sold Friday.
   Did Sunday's game sell out? _____

4. Brendan bought 4 box seats for $47.50 each. Then he bought 8 Section D tickets for $22.75 each. How much money did he spend?_____

More Variables

Use a variable to write an equation for each problem.
Then solve the problem.

1. The Panthers scored an unknown number of points in the first 6 games of the season. They then scored 539 points in the next 6 games. They scored a total of 1,187 for all 12 games. How many points did they score in the first 6 games?

   Equation: _____

   Answer: _____

2. Leah made 10 dozen beaded bracelets for the craft fair. She used a total of 960 beads for all the bracelets. She put an equal number of beads on each bracelet. What unknown number of beads is on each bracelet?

   Equation: _____

   Answer: _____

3. Halley read an unknown number of books over summer vacation. Each book had 42 pages. At the end of the summer, she had read 714 pages. How many books did Halley read?

   Equation: _____

   Answer: _____

4. Charlie counted 455 chocolate chips in the first bag. Charlie only counted 298 chocolate chips in the second bag. What mystery number of fewer chips did he count in the second bag than in the first bag?

   Equation: _____

   Answer: _____

In the Stars

Read the clues. Cross out the numbers in the stars to find the mystery number.

1. It's not 144 ÷ 3.

2. It's not 81 x 2.

3. It's not 115 – 23.

4. It's not 16 x 5.

5. It's not 150 ÷ 6.

6. It's not 39 + 72.

7. It's not 24 x 4.

8. It's not 38 x 3.

9. It's not 136 – 65

10. It's not 66 + 28.

48 114 92 25 96 80

162 94 111 98 71

The mystery number is _____.

Answer Key

Page 4
1. multiplication and addition; 138 legs
2. multiplication and addition; 280.6 pounds
3. subtraction and division; 4 animals

Page 5
1. $(5 + 5) \div 5 = 2$
2. $90 = 6 \times (3 + 12)$ or $(90 \div 6) - 3 = 12$
3. $120 - (20 \times 3) = 60$
4. $66 = (7 \times 8) + 10$
5. $(100 - 35) + 10 = 75$ or $100 - (35 - 10) = 75$
6. $(10 \div 2) \times 10 = 50$

Page 6
1. 824 miles; 2,987 miles
2. 600 miles; 1,800 miles
3. 5,920 feet; 4,245 feet
4. 390 miles; 775 miles

Page 7
1. Step 1: Find out how many scoops Jenna bought:
   $7 \times 3 = 21$
   Step 2: Multiply the number of scoops by 15¢ (or .15):
   $21 \times .15 = \$3.15$
   Answer: Jenna spent $3.15.
2. Step 1: Make equivalent fractions: $\frac{5}{10} \times \frac{2}{2} = \frac{10}{20}$
   Step 2: Compare Tessa's fraction to Josh's fraction:
   Tessa $\frac{10}{20}$, Josh $\frac{12}{20}$
   Answer: Josh used more sand.
3. Step 1: Find out how many minutes Lan surfed:
   $120 \div 2 = 60$ minutes
   Step 2: Find out how many minutes Biff surfed:
   $3 \times 60 = 180$ minutes
   Step 3: Compare Biff's, Lan's, and Corey's minutes: Biff 180, Lan 60, Corey 120
   Answer: Biff surfed the longest.

Page 8
1. $\frac{13}{12}$ or $1\frac{1}{12}$
2. $\frac{2}{3}$
3. 9 points
4. $\frac{3}{12}$ or $\frac{1}{4}$

Page 9
Gummy bears—chocolate chips, banana chips, candy sprinkles, hot caramel, peanuts, whipped cream
Chocolate chips—banana chips, candy sprinkles, hot caramel, peanuts, whipped cream
Banana chips—candy sprinkles, hot caramel, peanuts, whipped cream
Candy sprinkles—hot caramel, peanuts, whipped cream
Hot caramel—peanuts, whipped cream.
Peanuts—whipped cream.

Page 10
Chocolate Cupcakes

Ingredients	1 dozen	5 dozen	12 dozen	15 dozen
shortening	1 cup	5 cups	12 cups	15 cups
sugar	$1\frac{1}{3}$ cups	$6\frac{2}{3}$ cups	16 cups	20 cups
eggs	2	10	24	30
flour	$3\frac{1}{2}$ cups	$17\frac{1}{2}$ cups	42 cups	$52\frac{1}{2}$ cups
vanilla	2 tsp.	10 tsp.	24 tsp.	30 tsp.
baking soda	$1\frac{1}{4}$ tsp.	$6\frac{1}{4}$ tsp.	15 tsp.	$18\frac{3}{4}$ tsp.
chocolate chips	$1\frac{3}{4}$ cups	$8\frac{3}{4}$ cups	21 cups	$26\frac{1}{4}$ cups

Pink Lemonade

Ingredients	1 gallon	3 gallons	6 gallons	9 gallons
water	$5\frac{1}{2}$ cups	$16\frac{1}{2}$ cups	33 cups	$49\frac{1}{2}$ cups
sugar	$1\frac{2}{3}$ cups	5 cups	10 cups	15 cups
lemons	6	18	36	54
food coloring	$\frac{1}{4}$ tsp.	$\frac{3}{4}$ tsp.	$1\frac{1}{2}$ tsp.	$2\frac{1}{4}$ tsp.

Page 11
1. $(120 \div 12) \times 15 = 150$
2. $65 - (16 \times 3) = 17$
3. $(76 - 14) \div 2 = 31$
4. $72 = (12 \div 3) \times 18$ or $(72 \div 12) \times 3 = 18$
5. $20 + (8 \times 13) = 124$
6. $53 = 28 + (100 \div 4)$

Page 12
1. $\frac{1}{8}$
2. $\frac{4}{8}$ or $\frac{1}{2}$
3. $\frac{0}{6}$
4. $\frac{2}{6}$ or $\frac{1}{3}$
5. $\frac{4}{5}$
6. $\frac{1}{5}$
7. $\frac{2}{8}$ or $\frac{1}{4}$
8. $\frac{4}{8}$ or $\frac{1}{2}$

Page 13
1. 50
2. 50
3. $\frac{1}{2}$
4. $\frac{3}{4}$
5. 25%
6. 400

Page 14
1. 104
2. 10
3. $32.50, $4,225
4. 18%; snares: 18, kettles: 5, bass: 10, xylophone: 7

Page 15
1. $\frac{4}{10}$ or $\frac{2}{5}$; $\frac{5}{10}$ or $\frac{1}{2}$
2. $\frac{3}{8}$; $\frac{4}{8}$ or $\frac{1}{2}$, $\frac{1}{8}$
3. $\frac{4}{12}$ or $\frac{1}{3}$; $\frac{3}{12}$ or $\frac{1}{4}$, $\frac{0}{12}$ or 0

Page 16
1. No; the second shape is smaller.
2. Yes; they are the same size and shape.
3. No; they have a different number of sides.
4. Yes; they are the same size and shape.
5.
6.

Page 17
1. $793.50
2. $2,908.64
3. 10
4. $3,251

Page 18
1. 15.3 inches; 17.6 inches
2. 80°; 89°
3. 9.3 inches; 13.3 inches; 13.6 Inches

Page 19
1. Tanya; 2.1 seconds; 10.2 seconds
2. 1.6 meters; 1.6 meters
3. 94.7 points; 28.4 points

Page 20
Ariel: cheesecake
Anna: peach cobbler
Ashlee: sundae
Alicia: chocolate cake

Page 21
Baseball: 10; Football: 8
Tennis: 2; Soccer: 4
Basketball: 16

Pages 22–23
1. 60 ounces; 48 cups
2. 54 teaspoons; 18 teaspoons
3. 4 ounces; 3 pounds
4. 6 cups; 16 ounces
5. 136 ounces; 34 ounces
6. $4\frac{1}{2}$ tsp.; 10 pies

Page 24
1. 14
2. 18

Page 25
Tye, Jess, Aimee, Derek, Tammy, Carrie

Page 26
1. 7 hours, 35 minutes
2. 17 hours, 25 minutes
3. 8 hours, 25 minutes
4. 62 hours

Page 27
1.
10	3	2
0	8	7
5	4	6

2.
3	6	9
10	0	8
5	12	1

3.
4	13	3
5	7	8
11	0	9

4.
6	5	10
11	7	3
4	9	8

Pages 28–29
1. 3 hours, 33 minutes
2. 45 minutes
3. 4 hours, 30 minutes
4. 4 hours, 7 minutes
5. 2 hours, 15 minutes
6. 2 hours, 50 minutes
7. 3 hours, 25 minutes
8. 1 hour, 30 minutes

Pages 30–31

Date	Description	Debit	Deposit	Balance
8/12	Opened bank account		85.50	85.50
8/16	Allowance		13.75	99.25
8/28	Skateboard	35.99		63.26
9/12	School supplies	12.00		51.26
9/15	Clothes	24.55		26.71
9/19	Birthday check		20.00	46.71
10/5	Mom's watch	15.75		30.96
10/18	Helmet	14.50		16.46

1. $102.79   2. $119.25   3. $16.46

Answer Key

Page 32

1.
3	7	8
4	5	9
11	6	1

2.
5	11	8
9	12	3
10	1	13

3.
12	10	4
0	9	17
14	7	5

4.
14	11	1	8
9	16	6	3
7	2	12	13
4	5	15	10

Page 33

1. $4\frac{1}{2}$ brownies
2. $2\frac{2}{5}$
3. X, need to know how many teams there are altogether.
4. X, need to know all eight games' scores.

Page 34

Brett: skateboard
Hanna: ice cream
Scott: bike
Aaron: tennis shoes
Staci: watch

Page 35

24 games

Page 36

Dolphins: 48
Sea snakes: 6
Fish: 20
Sharks: 34
Jellyfish: 24
Seals: 16
Stingrays: 8
Starfish: 26
Eels: 18

Page 37

1. oval
2. octagon
3. equilateral triangle
4. square

Pages 38–39

1. Faith: 9.3; Sun City: 46.1
   Junction: 102.3; Danville: 129.7
   Mountville: 333; Chaney: 408.5
2. 306.2 miles
3. 323.7 miles
4. 83.6 miles
5. 641.2 miles
6. 208.4 miles
7. 599.4 miles

Page 40

1. $\frac{10}{20} + \frac{7}{10} = 1\frac{1}{5}$
2. $\frac{4}{6} + \frac{5}{9} = 1\frac{2}{9}$

3. $\frac{7}{8} + \frac{9}{12} = 1\frac{5}{8}$
4. $\frac{8}{18} + \frac{4}{6} = 1\frac{5}{8}$

Page 41

Anh biking

Hassan cooking

Nicki singing

Hector mountain climbing

Page 42

1.
108	9
144	12
36	3
132	11

rule: ÷ 12

2.
3	18
45	60
37	52
15	30

rule: + 15

3.
5	100
20	400
8	160
3	60

rule: x 20

4.
99	86
26	13
50	37
35	22

rule: −13

Page 43

Pool A: 106 feet; Pool B: 77 feet
Pool C: 146 feet; Pool D: 120 feet
Pool B; it is the only pool small enough to fit.

Pages 44–45

1. Cougars; Cougars: 33, Warriors: 30
2. 25 yards; 25%
3. 34 yards; the Warrior's 34 yard line
4. Cougars; Warriors; Cougars: 37, Warriors: 38
5. No; 9 yards
6. 290 yards; 20 points

Pages 46–47

1. Daisy, 9.2 miles, 119.1 miles
2. 64.1 miles, Wheeler and Mt. Ridge
3. 284 miles, 8.4 gallons
4. The way there, 1.5 miles, 222.1 miles

Page 48

1. flower garden; 98.4 sq. ft.; 8.3 sq. ft.; 280.3 sq. ft.

2. Classroom D; 1620 sq. ft.; Classroom B; 850.5 sq. ft.; 4,945.5 sq. ft.
3. purple scarf; 360 sq. in.; 118.5 sq. in.; 1,154.5 sq. in.

Page 49

36 games

Pages 50–51

1. Girls; 10 tickets
2. 30 tickets
3. Wednesday and Sunday
4. Monday; 45 tickets
5. Friday and Saturday
6. $1,175
7. Dogs: $528.75; Cats: $411.25, Rabbits: $235.00

Page 52

Ruby Red: purple grape, ocean blue, leafy green, sunny yellow, cheeky pink, chocolate brown, burnt orange, black cat
Purple Grape: ocean blue, leafy green, sunny yellow, cheeky pink, chocolate brown, burnt orange, black cat
Ocean Blue: leafy green, sunny yellow, cheeky pink, chocolate brown, burnt orange, black cat
Leafy Green: sunny yellow, cheeky pink, chocolate brown, burnt orange, black cat
Sunny Yellow: cheeky pink, chocolate brown, burnt orange, black cat
Cheeky Pink: chocolate brown, burnt orange, black cat
Chocolate Brown: burnt orange, black cat
Burnt Orange: black cat
36 fun color combinations are available.

Page 53

1. Tanner, Randy, Kevin, Dylan, Brian
2. 4 feet, 0 inches
3. 6 feet, 3 inches
4. 3 inches
5. 2 feet, 3 inches
6. 26 feet

Pages 54–55

List 1: Spike; List 2: Prissy;
List 3: Rocky; List 4: Mouse;
List 5: Sheena; List 6: Thor
1. $1.81
2. $24.57
3. $5.43

Page 56

1. Shane; Grant; $\frac{9}{20}$; $2\frac{19}{40}$;

Shane, Tyler, Brent, Grant
2. Justin; Erin; 19.6 points; 251.8 points Erin, Shana, Myra, Justin

Page 57

1.
13	25
22	34
3	15
30	42
65	77

rule: +12

2.
15	60
9	36
12	48
20	80
11	44

rule: x 4

3.
10	12
11	15
12	18
13	21
14	24

rule: + even numbers 2–10

4.
6	18
8	40
9	63
11	99
13	143

rule: x odd numbers 3–11

Page 58

1. 18n = 486; his car got 27 miles per gallon.
2. 1,408 + n = 1,595; Melissa scored 187 more points.
3. 30n = 360 miles; Mia traveled to and from work for 12 days.
4. 21n = 504; there were 24 pictures on each roll of film.

Page 59

1. 13,956 seats
2. 14,373 seats
3. No
4. $372

Page 60

1. 539 + n = 1,187 points; they scored 648 points in the first six games.
2. 120n = 960; there are 8 beads on each bracelet.
3. 42n = 714; Halley read 17 books.
4. 455 – n = 298; Charlie counted 157 less chips in the second bag.

Page 61

The mystery number is 98.

Nice work,

_____!
(Name)

You're a
problem solving
champion!